First English-language edition published 1986 in the U.K. by
Hodder and Stoughton
This U.S. edition published 1986 by Derrydale Books, distributed
by Crown Publishers, Inc.

Library of Congress Cataloging-in-Publication Data

Scarry, Huck.
    Things that sail.

    Translation of: Lo sai come si naviga?
    Summary: Depicts ships through the ages and presents
scientific principles of why things float and sail.
    1. Ships – Juvenile literature.   2. Navigation –
Juvenile literature.   [1. Navigation.   2. Ships]
I. Title
VM150.S28   1986   623.8   85-31193
ISBN 0-517-61656-4

h g f e d c b a

Printed in Spain by Artes Gràficas Toledo S.A.
D. L. TO: 332-1986

Huck Scarry
Things that
Sail

Derrydale Books
New York

Earth's Natural Highway

Although almost everyone on Earth lives on dry land, most of our planet's surface is covered by water. Seen from space, the Earth looks blue, which is why it is sometimes called the Blue Planet.

A sailor from any port on Earth can reach any other port, anywhere in the world, by sailing across the sea, Earth's natural highway.

Roads and railways crisscross the world, but they are a very modern means of travel and transport. A couple of hundred years ago there were no railways, and the roads were often no more than bumpy, muddy tracks. For hundreds of years the best way to travel was by water. This is why most of the world's large cities are at the edge of the sea or on the banks of a great river.

The civilization which grew up in ancient Egypt, three and a half thousand years ago, depended on the Nile River. Around the towns, the temples, the pyramids and the fields, lay desert. The river was the highway which linked the towns together. Other ancient civilizations grew up on the banks of the Tigris and the Euphrates in Asia, the Indus and the Ganges in India, and the Yellow River in China.

Three thousand years later, when men set out from Europe to search for new lands across the sea, they went by ship. They explored the great continents of Africa, Asia, North and South America and, eventually, Australia, by sailing up the rivers that led into the unknown lands.

Thousands of years ago, when people first began to build settlements to live in, boats and ships were the best and safest way of traveling from place to place, and the rivers and the sea were their natural highways.

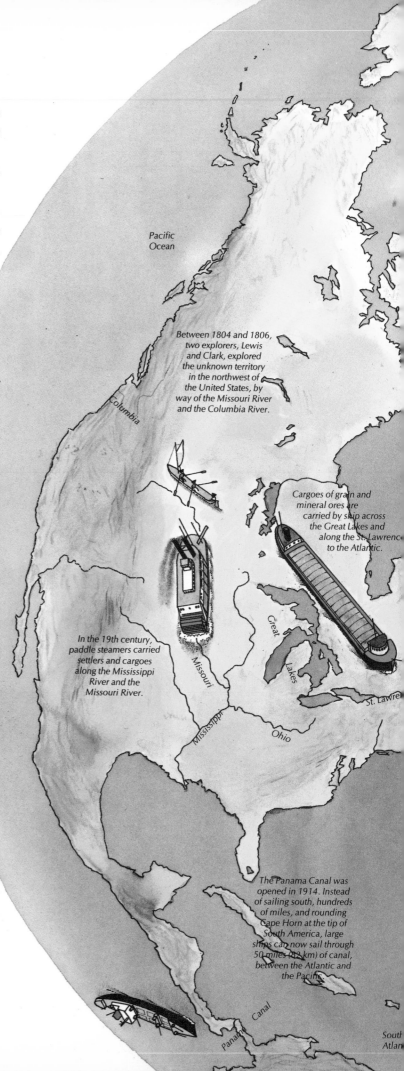

Pacific Ocean

Between 1804 and 1806, two explorers, Lewis and Clark, explored the unknown territory in the northwest of the United States, by way of the Missouri River and the Columbia River.

Columbia

Cargoes of grain and mineral ores are carried by ship across the Great Lakes and along the St. Lawrence to the Atlantic.

In the 19th century, paddle steamers carried settlers and cargoes along the Mississippi River and the Missouri River.

Great Lakes

St. Lawrence

Missouri

Mississippi

Ohio

The Panama Canal was opened in 1914. Instead of sailing south, hundreds of miles, and rounding Cape Horn at the tip of South America, large ships can now sail through 50 miles (82 km) of canal, between the Atlantic and the Pacific.

Panama Canal

South Atlantic

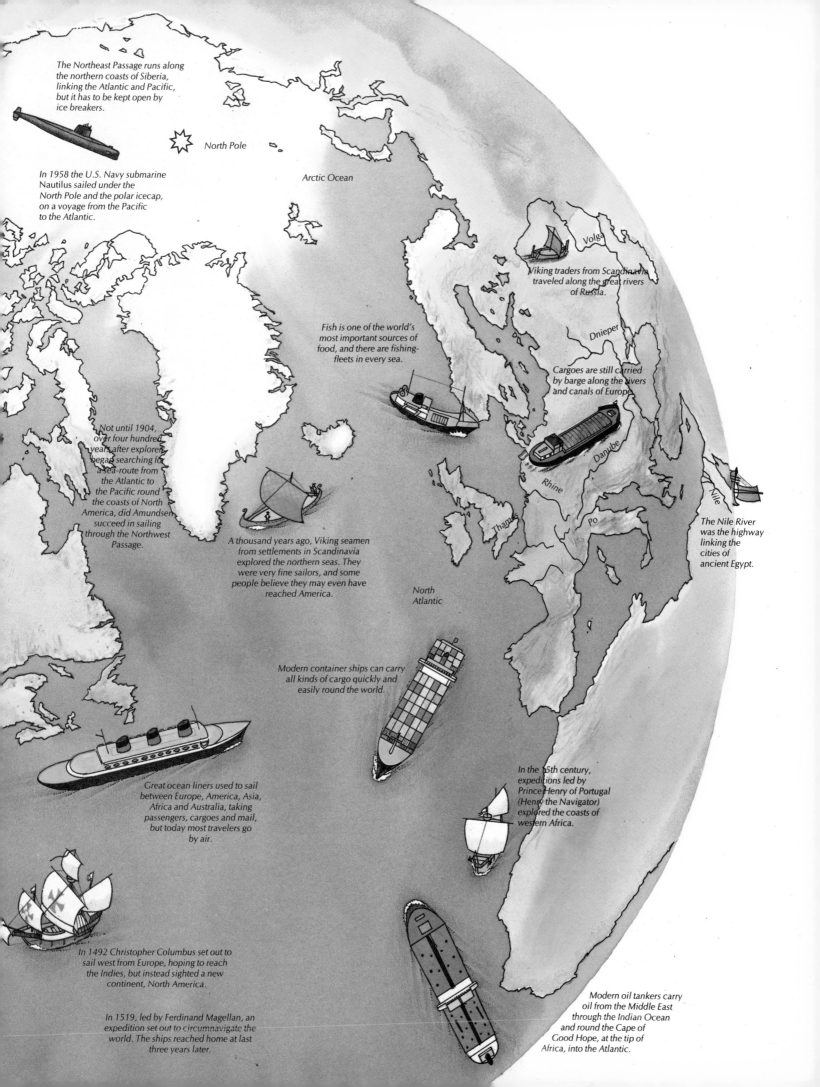

The Northeast Passage runs along the northern coasts of Siberia, linking the Atlantic and Pacific, but it has to be kept open by ice breakers.

In 1958 the U.S. Navy submarine *Nautilus* sailed under the North Pole and the polar icecap, on a voyage from the Pacific to the Atlantic.

North Pole

Arctic Ocean

Viking traders from Scandinavia traveled along the great rivers of Russia.

Volga

Dnieper

Fish is one of the world's most important sources of food, and there are fishing-fleets in every sea.

Cargoes are still carried by barge along the rivers and canals of Europe.

Danube

Rhine

Po

Thames

Nile

The Nile River was the highway linking the cities of ancient Egypt.

Not until 1904, over four hundred years after explorers began searching for a sea-route from the Atlantic to the Pacific round the coasts of North America, did Amundsen succeed in sailing through the Northwest Passage.

A thousand years ago, Viking seamen from settlements in Scandinavia explored the northern seas. They were very fine sailors, and some people believe they may even have reached America.

North Atlantic

Modern container ships can carry all kinds of cargo quickly and easily round the world.

Great ocean liners used to sail between Europe, America, Asia, Africa and Australia, taking passengers, cargoes and mail, but today most travelers go by air.

In the 15th century, expeditions led by Prince Henry of Portugal (Henry the Navigator) explored the coasts of western Africa.

In 1492 Christopher Columbus set out to sail west from Europe, hoping to reach the Indies, but instead sighted a new continent, North America.

In 1519, led by Ferdinand Magellan, an expedition set out to circumnavigate the world. The ships reached home at last three years later.

Modern oil tankers carry oil from the Middle East through the Indian Ocean and round the Cape of Good Hope, at the tip of Africa, into the Atlantic.

More than two thousand years ago, a Greek scientist called Archimedes made a discovery. He was trying to think of a way of checking whether a crown made for the king was pure gold, or gold mixed with a cheaper metal. He stepped into a bath tub full of water, and the tub overflowed. Archimedes jumped out of the tub and ran through the streets shouting, "Eureka! Eureka", which means "I have found it! I have found it!" What had he found?

Ευρηκα
"Eureka!"

Archimedes' Principle

When an object is immersed in water, it pushes aside, or displaces, enough water to make room for itself, and the volume of displaced water equals the volume of the object. If you weigh the object, and then immerse it in water and weigh it again, it loses weight, and the weight it loses equals the weight of water it displaces.

Archimedes immersed the crown, to discover what volume of metal it contained. He then immersed a lump of gold weighing the same as the crown, and it displaced a different volume of water. The crown was not pure gold.

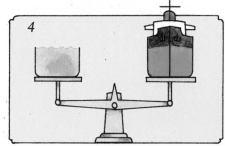

(1) Consider the case of a ship.
(2) The ship displaces water.
(3) The volume of water displaced equals the volume of the part of the ship that is immersed.

(4) The weight of water displaced equals the weight of the part of the ship below the waterline.
(5) Because the total volume of the ship is greater than the volume of water displaced, it floats.

To test Archimedes' Principle, take a paper cup, a measuring cup, and a precise weighing machine, such as a scale.

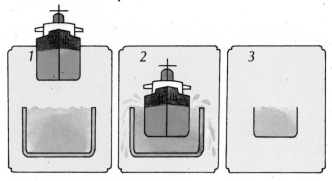

Pour 8 ounces of water into the measuring cup.

Pour 4 ounces of water into the paper cup.

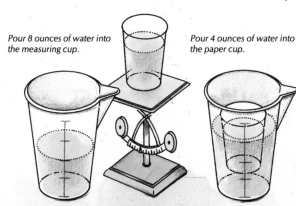

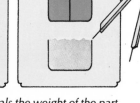

Lower the paper cup carefully into the measuring cup. How many ounces of water does it displace?

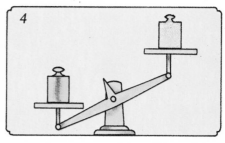

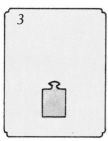

If you immerse a lump of metal in water, the volume of water it displaces equals its own volume; but the lump of metal weighs more than the water, so it sinks.

If, however, you hammer the lump of metal into a dish shape, it will float, and the water it displaces will weigh more than it does.

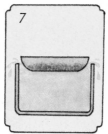

The weight and volume of a ship are measured in tonnage. Displacement tonnage is the total weight of a ship and everything on board; gross register tonnage, the ship's capacity; deadweight tonnage, the weight of the cargo, stores and fuel; net register tonnage, the ship's capacity for carrying cargo and passengers.

Loading levels are painted on the side of a cargo ship. There are different levels for different climates and seasons. When the ship is fully loaded, the appropriate mark should be at or above water level. Samuel Plimsoll brought in the first such line, the Plimsoll Mark, in 1876, to protect the lives of seamen.

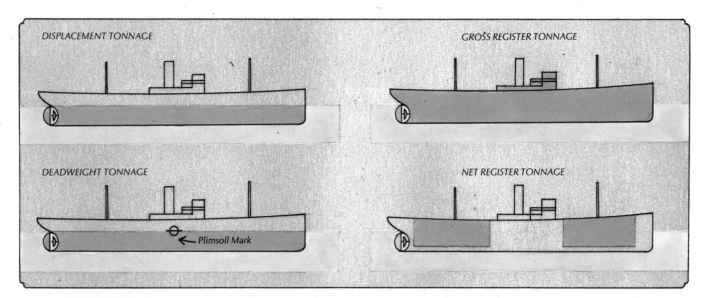

DISPLACEMENT TONNAGE

GROSS REGISTER TONNAGE

DEADWEIGHT TONNAGE

← Plimsoll Mark

NET REGISTER TONNAGE

The lines on the left are the loading lines for wooden ships.

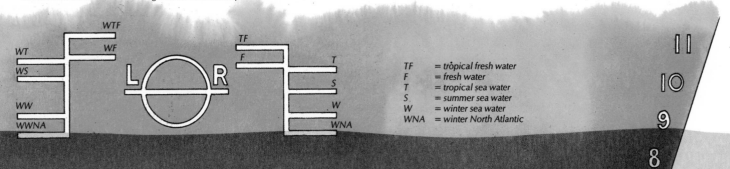

WTF
WT
WF
WS
WW
WWNA

TF
F
T
S
W
WNA

L O R

TF = tropical fresh water
F = fresh water
T = tropical sea water
S = summer sea water
W = winter sea water
WNA = winter North Atlantic

11
10
9
8
7
6

The capital letters on either side of the Plimsoll Mark show where the ship is registered.
LR = Lloyd's Register (Great Britain)

The scale shows in meters or feet how much of the hull is below the waterline.

Primitive Boats

For thousands of years, people built simple boats, using any materials that came to hand and that would float. These boats were not very stable, but the people who built and used them were often ingenious and skillful.

Eskimo hunters used kayaks, made of animal skins stretched over a frame of bone or wood.

Basket-shaped coracles were built in Ireland and Wales, with animal skins stretched over a framework of laths, and sealed with pitch to make them waterproof.

The Red Indians of North America built slender birchbark canoes which they paddled swiftly and skillfully along rushing rivers.

A dug-out canoe, made by hollowing out a log, is simple to build but apt to tip over when it is being paddled along.

AMERICA

Amazon

Boats built from bundles of reeds tied together, and with sails made of reeds, are still used on Lake Titicaca.

The jangada raft, with its triangular sail, is used by fishermen in Brazil. The centerboard makes it more stable.

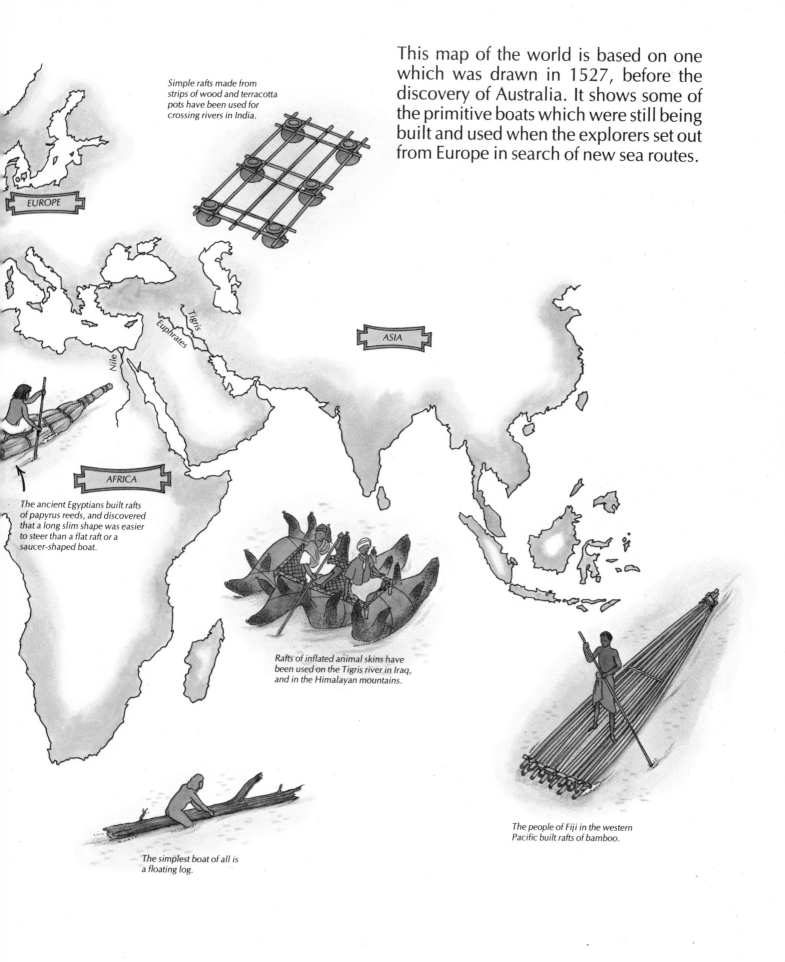

This map of the world is based on one which was drawn in 1527, before the discovery of Australia. It shows some of the primitive boats which were still being built and used when the explorers set out from Europe in search of new sea routes.

Simple rafts made from strips of wood and terracotta pots have been used for crossing rivers in India.

EUROPE

ASIA

AFRICA

Nile

Euphrates

Tigris

The ancient Egyptians built rafts of papyrus reeds, and discovered that a long slim shape was easier to steer than a flat raft or a saucer-shaped boat.

Rafts of inflated animal skins have been used on the Tigris river in Iraq, and in the Himalayan mountains.

The people of Fiji in the western Pacific built rafts of bamboo.

The simplest boat of all is a floating log.

Water Sleds

Boats and ships don't run on wheels. A boat slides through the water on its hull, rather like someone tobogganing down a slope.

Mast

Movable hatches cover the hold.

Cabin

It is easy to punt a boat through shallow water by pushing the long punt poles against the riverbed.

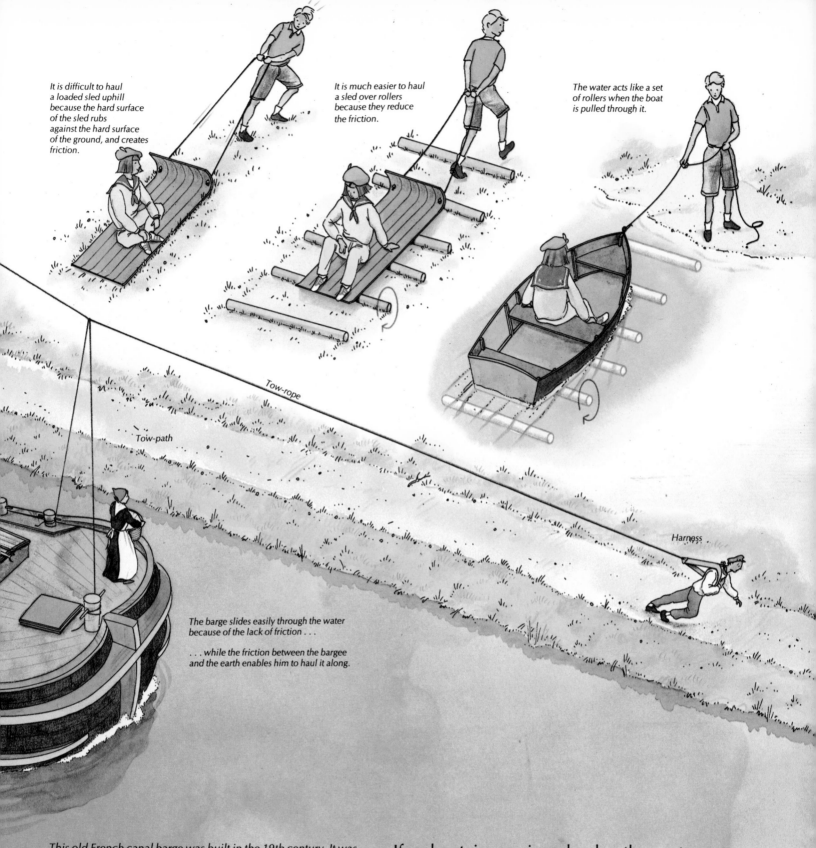

It is difficult to haul a loaded sled uphill because the hard surface of the sled rubs against the hard surface of the ground, and creates friction.

It is much easier to haul a sled over rollers because they reduce the friction.

The water acts like a set of rollers when the boat is pulled through it.

Tow-rope

Tow-path

Harness

The barge slides easily through the water because of the lack of friction . . .

. . . while the friction between the bargee and the earth enables him to haul it along.

This old French canal barge was built in the 19th century. It was over 124 feet (38 meters) long. Normally such barges were towed by teams of horses, but one man, working alone, could tow the barge if need be, though when fully loaded it weighed over 280 tons.

If a boat is moving slowly, the water offers little resistance. Water molecules glide easily over one another, and a boat slides over them almost effortlessly. And as a boat displaces its own weight when it floats on water, one man, working alone, can haul a barge carrying a load of several hundred tons.

Oars and Sails

When a boat is on the open water, it has to be propelled forward, or it will drift helplessly. One of the simplest ways of doing this is to row, using oars.

Effort *Resistance* *Lever* *Fulcrum* *Resistance* *Lever* *Fulcrum*

An oar is a lever. By exerting strength at one end of a lever, you can move a much greater weight, or overcome a much greater resistance, than you could deal with on your own. A rower uses the oars as a pair of levers, and drives the boat forward, stroke by stroke.

The mast is lowered, and the sail stowed on deck, when not in use.

In ancient times, galley slaves had to row ships in the Mediterranean Sea. It was hard, inhuman work. Sometimes, if they were lucky and the wind was blowing in the right direction, a sail could be hoisted so that the wind's strength drove the ship along, but any change of direction brought the oars out again.

These two ships were built in ancient Egypt, during the reign of Sahure (2540–2421 B.C.). The eye painted on the ship's prow is to help her "see" the way. The thick cord running from the prow to the stern, over the crutches, helped to strengthen the hull in high seas which could have broken her back.

Direction of the wind

The ship is steered by using the upright oars at the stern.

When a fresh breeze blows from the stern, it pushes the boat forward through the water.

Wings and Sails

Air passing over the upper surface of the airplane's wing has to travel faster because of the curved shape. This means that the air particles are spread out more thinly, and the pressure is less. The air below the wing is moving more slowly, over a shorter distance, so its pressure is greater.

A bird's wing, the wings of an airplane, and the sail on a sailboat, are similar in shape. They are all airfoils. The upper, or outer, surface is curved. This means that the air particles must travel faster across it, so that they are spread more thinly. There is less air pressure on the upper surface of the wing, or the outer surface of the sail, than there is on the lower or inner surface. The higher pressure below the wing lifts the bird or airplane into the air, and the higher pressure on the concave side of the sail drives the boat through the water.

Imagine a pair of sails laid flat, like wings. As they fill with wind, they take on the same curved shape as the wings of an airplane. The sail is filled by a cushion of wind and acts like the other airfoils.

Fast air (generating lift)

Slow air

To test the airfoil effect for yourself, take a piece of thin, light paper, and hold it so that it hangs down from your hand, at about the level of your lower lip. If you blow fast and hard, reducing the air pressure, what happens?

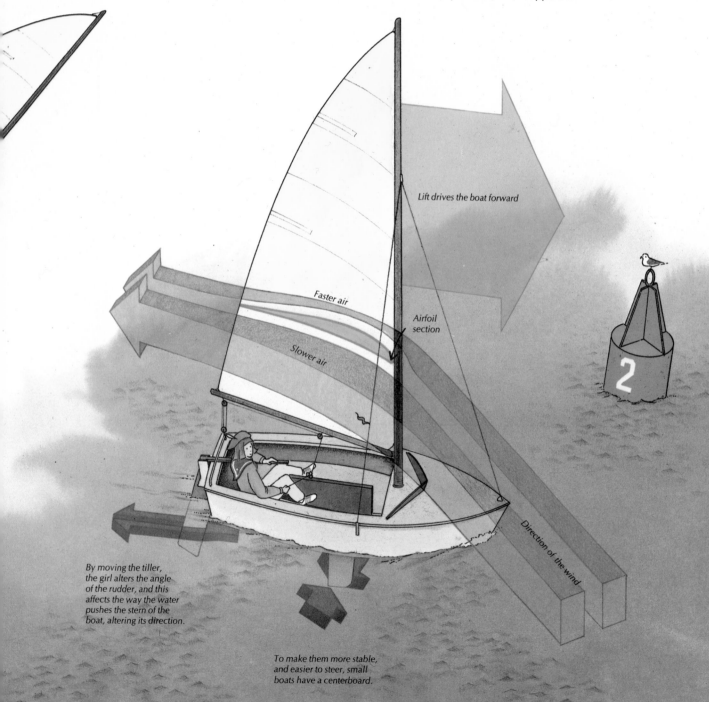

Lift drives the boat forward

Faster air

Airfoil section

Slower air

Direction of the wind

By moving the tiller, the girl alters the angle of the rudder, and this affects the way the water pushes the stern of the boat, altering its direction.

To make them more stable, and easier to steer, small boats have a centerboard.

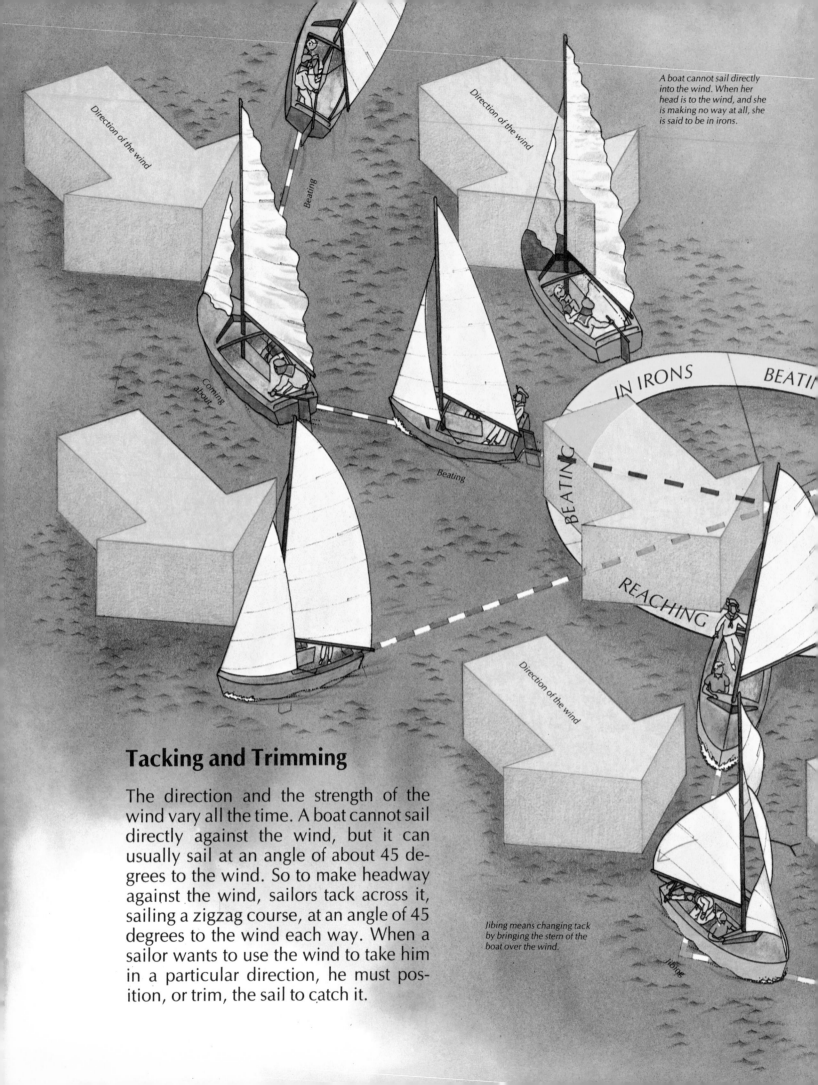

Direction of the wind

Direction of the wind

Beating

Coming about

Beating

A boat cannot sail directly into the wind. When her head is to the wind, and she is making no way at all, she is said to be in irons.

IN IRONS

BEATING

BEATING

REACHING

Direction of the wind

Beating

Jibing means changing tack by bringing the stern of the boat over the wind.

Jibing

Tacking and Trimming

The direction and the strength of the wind vary all the time. A boat cannot sail directly against the wind, but it can usually sail at an angle of about 45 degrees to the wind. So to make headway against the wind, sailors tack across it, sailing a zigzag course, at an angle of 45 degrees to the wind each way. When a sailor wants to use the wind to take him in a particular direction, he must position, or trim, the sail to catch it.

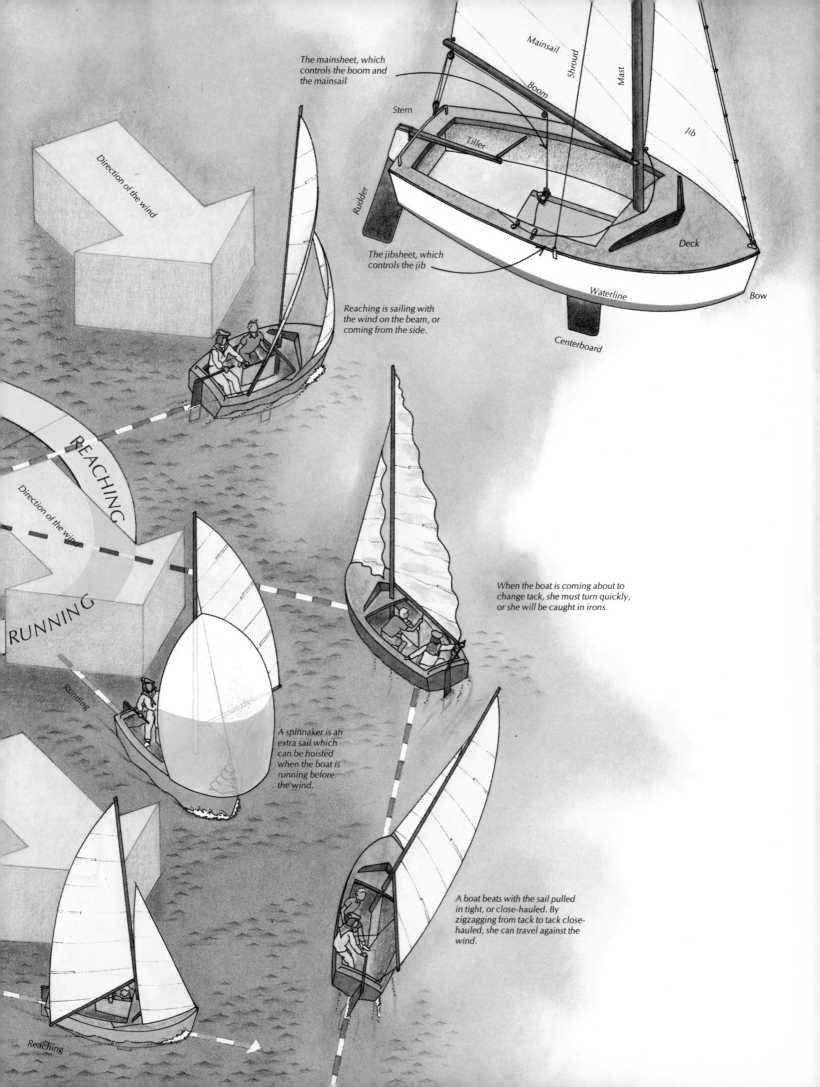

The mainsheet, which controls the boom and the mainsail

Mainsail

Shroud

Boom

Mast

Stern

Jib

Tiller

Rudder

Deck

The jibsheet, which controls the jib

Waterline

Bow

Centerboard

Direction of the wind

Reaching is sailing with the wind on the beam, or coming from the side.

REACHING

Direction of the wind

RUNNING

Running

When the boat is coming about to change tack, she must turn quickly, or she will be caught in irons.

A spinnaker is an extra sail which can be hoisted when the boat is running before the wind.

A boat beats with the sail pulled in tight, or close-hauled. By zigzagging from tack to tack close-hauled, she can travel against the wind.

Reaching

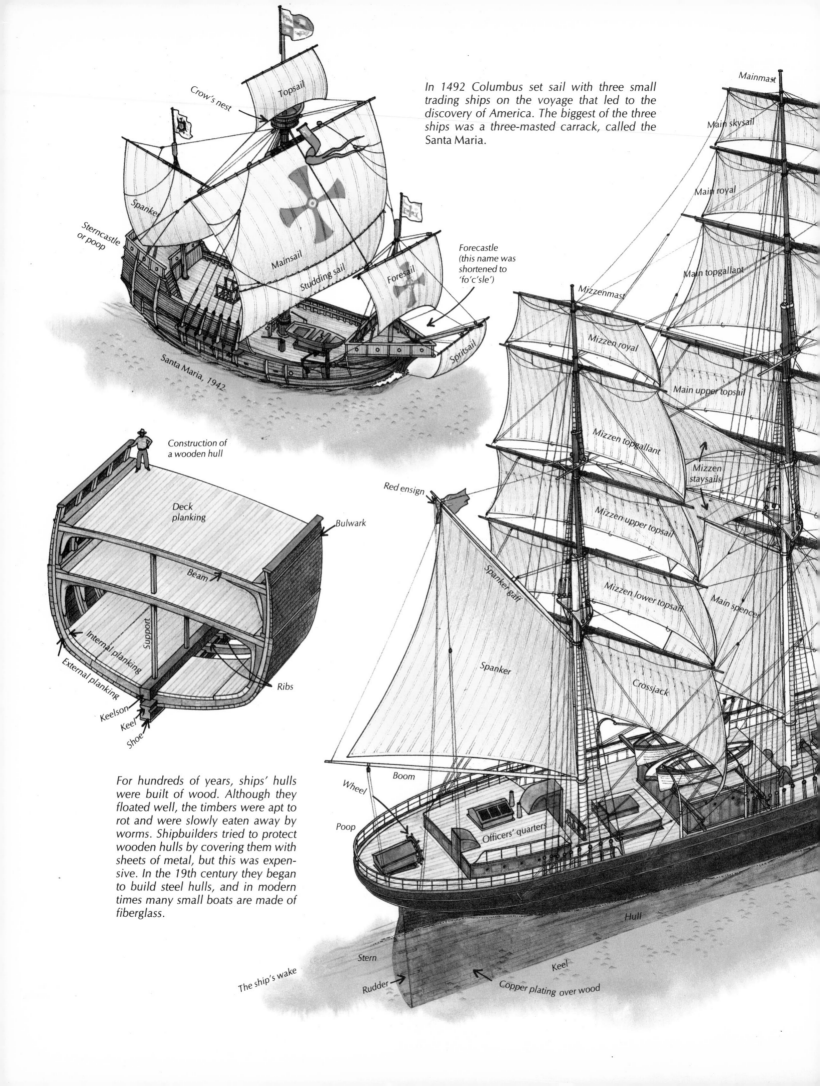

Crow's nest

Topsail

Spanker

Sterncastle or poop

Mainsail

Studding sail

Foresail

Forecastle (this name was shortened to 'fo'c'sle')

Spritsail

Santa Maria, 1942

In 1492 Columbus set sail with three small trading ships on the voyage that led to the discovery of America. The biggest of the three ships was a three-masted carrack, called the Santa Maria.

Construction of a wooden hull

Deck planking

Bulwark

Beam

Internal planking

Support

External planking

Keelson

Keel

Shoe

Ribs

For hundreds of years, ships' hulls were built of wood. Although they floated well, the timbers were apt to rot and were slowly eaten away by worms. Shipbuilders tried to protect wooden hulls by covering them with sheets of metal, but this was expensive. In the 19th century they began to build steel hulls, and in modern times many small boats are made of fiberglass.

Mainmast

Main skysail

Main royal

Main topgallant

Mizzenmast

Mizzen royal

Main upper topsail

Mizzen topgallant

Mizzen staysails

Red ensign

Mizzen upper topsail

Spanker gaff

Main spencer

Mizzen lower topsail

Spanker

Crossjack

Boom

Wheel

Poop

Officers' quarters

Stern

The ship's wake

Rudder

Copper plating over wood

Keel

Hull

Sailing Ships

On a sailing ship, every sail, every rope, every piece of equipment, has its own name. The three ships shown on these pages are drawn to about the same scale. They cover 450 years of the history of sail: the *Santa Maria* from the days when men were setting out on long, dangerous voyages in search of new sea-routes and new lands; the *Cutty Sark* from the time when a swift passage was the thing that mattered most and every inch of canvas counted; and the *Rainbow*, a fast and elegant racing yacht.

Foremast

Yardarm

Fore royal

Fore topgallant

Main staysails

Fore upper topsail

Flying jib

Fore lower topsail

Jib

Jib boom

Fore staysail

Main lower topsail

Fore course or foresail

Bowsprit

Figurehead

Hatch

Fo'c'sle (crew's quarters)

in course mainsail

Deck house

Cutwater

Bow

Cutty Sark, launched in Aberdeen (Scotland) in 1869

Cargo of tea in the hold

In 1887–8, the clipper Cutty Sark carried a cargo of wool from Australia to Great Britain in 69 days—a clear month shorter than the average sailing time.

Spreaders

Aluminium mast

J 4

Battens

Mainsail

Jibstay

Shrouds

Jib

Flying jib

Lifebelts

Stern

Rudder

Keel

Rainbow, a J-class racing sloop which won the America's Cup in 1934.

Hull (bronze plating over steel)

Bow

Some Sailing Ships

Trading ships like this one sailed the North Sea in the 13th and 14th centuries. In place of the steering oar there was now a rudder, hinged to the sternpost of the ship.

Trading ship, 13th century

Viking longship about AD 1000

The Vikings' steer-board, or steering oar, gave us the word starboard which is still used for the right-hand side of a ship. The left-hand is the port side.

This 12-meter racer competed for the America's Cup, the most famous yachting trophy of our day.

Weatherly, USA, 1962

The 19th century clipper ships carried cargo and passengers at a fast clip—bringing tea and spices from the Orient and wool from Australia, and taking prospectors to join the Gold Rush in California.

Republic, USA, 1800

The Mayflower crossed the Atlantic in 66 days, carrying the Pilgrim Fathers to found their first settlement in America.

Chinese junk, about 1900

Oriental junks have sailed the coasts and seas of eastern Asia for centuries. Their paneled sails are stiffened with slats of bamboo.

Mayflower, England, 1620

Elsie, USA, 1910

S-class, USA

Schooners were developed in America in the 19th century. Elsie was a fishing vessel and fished the Grand Banks off Newfoundland.

Today, most people who go sailing choose small sail-boats. Sailing has become a sport. These small, lively, pleasure craft are sailed for fun.

Thistle, USA

Paddles

The paddles which canoeists use are similar in shape to the duck's feet.

A duck uses its webbed feet to paddle its way through the water.

In 1736 an Englishman called Jonathan Hull designed a steam-driven tugboat with two paddle wheels. The boat was probably never built, for the steam engines of the time were far from practical.

Sailing ships depend entirely on the wind, but its direction and force vary all the time. If it begins to blow dangerously hard, so that it may rip the sails, snap the rigging and even break the mast, the sailors must shorten sail by reefing, or take down the sails altogether. If the wind drops, on the other hand, the ship may be becalmed.

For centuries, water mills have harnessed the force of rushing water by using it to turn a water wheel which is linked to the millstones. The invention of the steam engine led to experiments with steam-driven paddle wheels, as a way of driving ships along.

Continuing improvements in the design and construction of paddle wheels have made this a much more efficient means of propulsion.

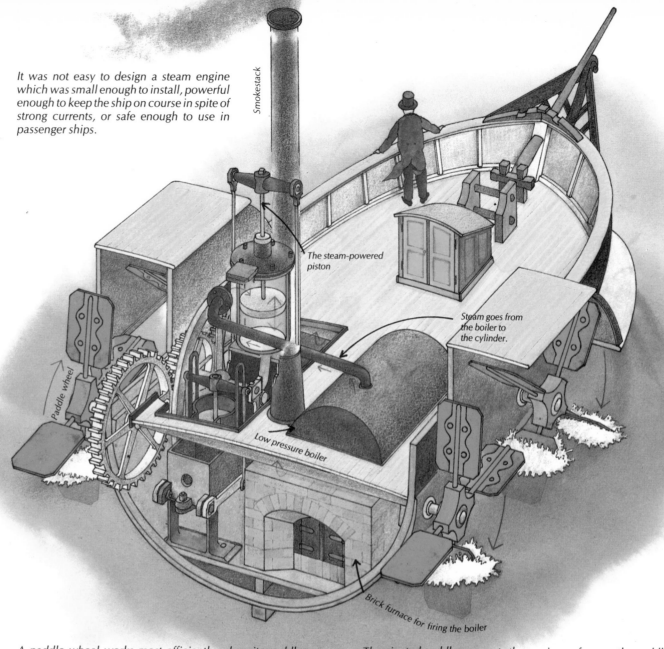

It was not easy to design a steam engine which was small enough to install, powerful enough to keep the ship on course in spite of strong currents, or safe enough to use in passenger ships.

Smokestack

The steam-powered piston

Steam goes from the boiler to the cylinder.

Paddle wheel

Low pressure boiler

Brick furnace for firing the boiler

A paddle wheel works most efficiently when its paddles are pivoted to bite the water.

The pivoted paddles generate the maximum force as the paddle wheel turns.

Wheel rim

Paddle mounted on pivoting arm

Connecting arm

Driving arm

Axle

Eccentric crown wheels

Propellers

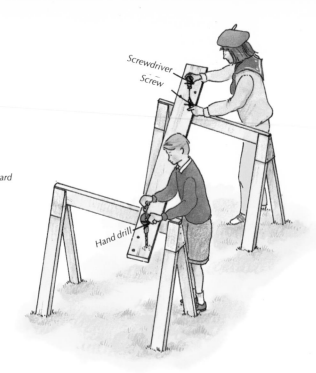

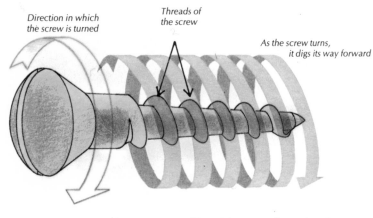

Direction in which the screw is turned

Threads of the screw

As the screw turns, it digs its way forward

Screwdriver

Screw

Hand drill

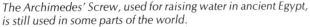

The Archimedes' Screw, used for raising water in ancient Egypt, is still used in some parts of the world.

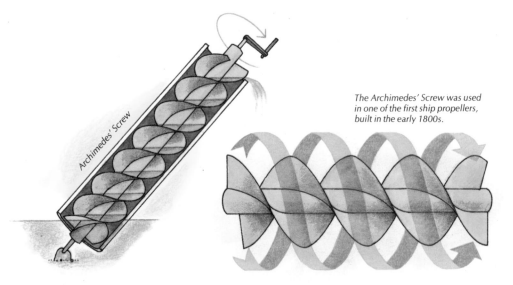

Archimedes' Screw

The Archimedes' Screw was used in one of the first ship propellers, built in the early 1800s.

The Archimedes' Screw was being used to raise water in ancient Egypt, four thousand years ago. It was enclosed in a close fitting, watertight cylinder. The machine was turned by hand, and as the screw rotated, water was wound up it and spilled out at the top.

A propeller works like a screw, or like the bit of a drill, digging its way forwards as it spins. Today almost all ships are driven by propellers.

Which was better, a paddle or a propeller? The argument started in 1816, when the first propeller-driven ship was built, and went on until 1845, when the Admiralty held a contest between HMS *Rattler*, which was propeller-driven, and HMS *Alecto*, a paddle-sloop. The ships were tied together, stern to stern, and then the signal to start was given. *Rattler* towed *Alecto* astern, winning the tug of war every time.

The Admiralty meant to be fair. They chose two ships of about the same size, and staged the race in calm water. But it is right to add that the moment of starting is always the moment of least efficiency where paddle wheels are concerned.

HMS Alecto

HMS Rattler

Modern propellers may have two, three, four, five or more blades. They are designed for maximum efficiency. The shape of the blades is designed to suit the work they have to do.

The number and the shape of the blades in a marine propeller depend on the speed and purpose for which the ship is designed.

A propeller for a merchant or passenger ship, which is not likely to achieve very high speeds, has fewer and broader blades.

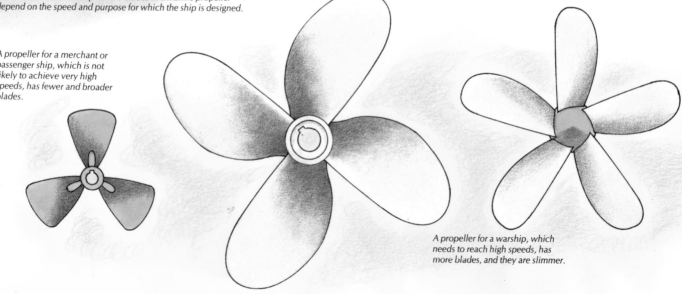

A propeller for a warship, which needs to reach high speeds, has more blades, and they are slimmer.

Steamships

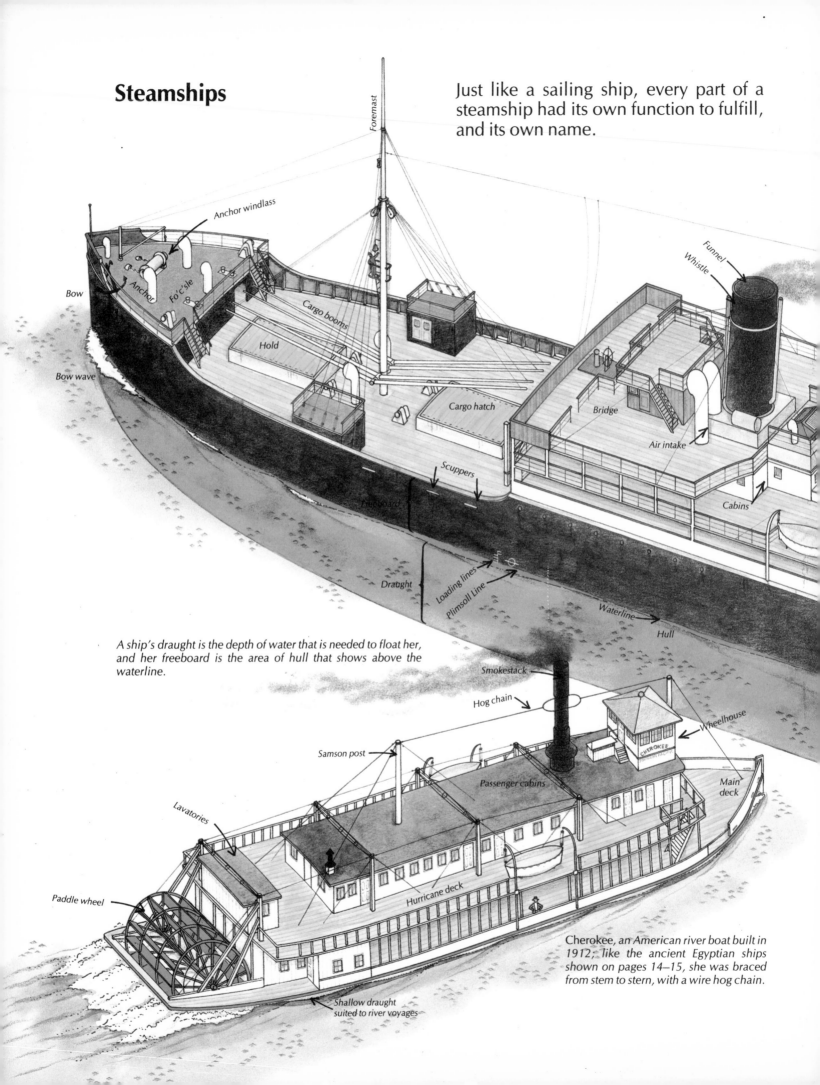

Just like a sailing ship, every part of a steamship had its own function to fulfill, and its own name.

Foremast

Anchor windlass

Funnel

Whistle

Bow

Anchor

Fo'c'sle

Cargo booms

Hold

Cargo hatch

Bridge

Air intake

Cabins

Bow wave

Scuppers

Freeboard

Draught

Loading lines

Plimsoll Line

Waterline

Hull

A ship's draught is the depth of water that is needed to float her, and her freeboard is the area of hull that shows above the waterline.

Smokestack

Hog chain

Wheelhouse

Samson post

Passenger cabins

Main deck

Lavatories

Paddle wheel

Hurricane deck

Cherokee, an American river boat built in 1912; like the ancient Egyptian ships shown on pages 14–15, she was braced from stem to stern, with a wire hog chain.

Shallow draught suited to river voyages

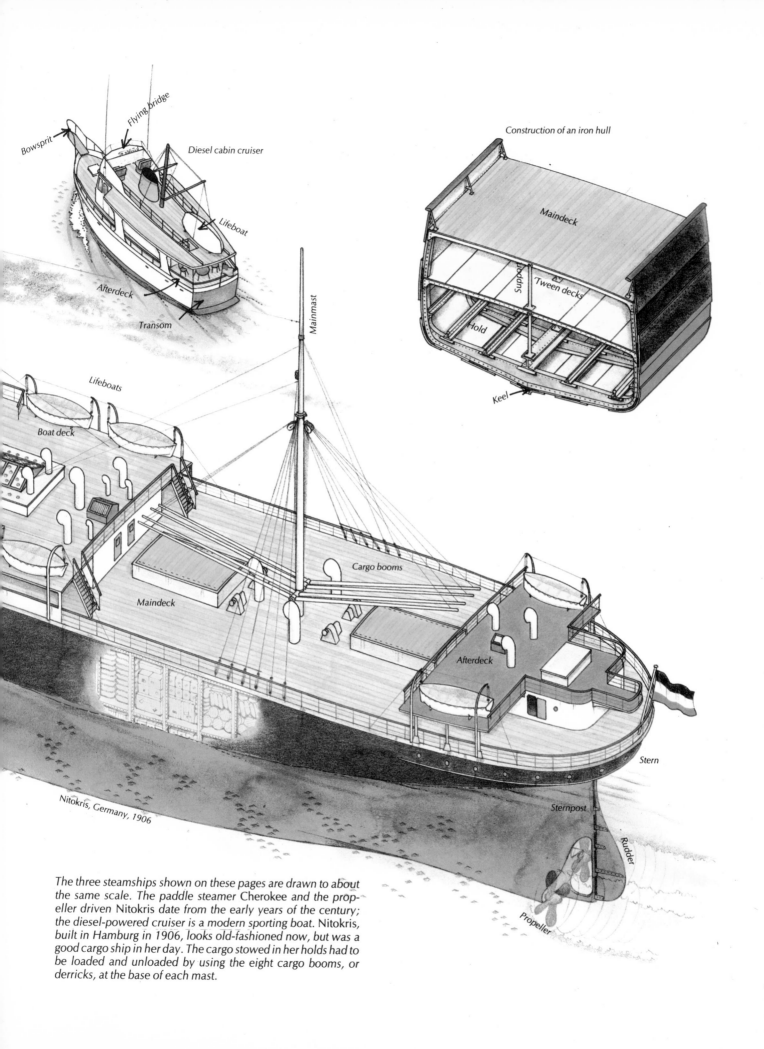

Flying bridge

Bowsprit

Diesel cabin cruiser

Lifeboat

Afterdeck

Transom

Construction of an iron hull

Maindeck

Support

'Tween decks

Hold

Keel

Mainmast

Lifeboats

Boat deck

Cargo booms

Maindeck

Afterdeck

Stern

Sternpost

Nitokris, Germany, 1906

Rudder

Propeller

The three steamships shown on these pages are drawn to about the same scale. The paddle steamer Cherokee and the propeller driven Nitokris date from the early years of the century; the diesel-powered cruiser is a modern sporting boat. Nitokris, built in Hamburg in 1906, looks old-fashioned now, but was a good cargo ship in her day. The cargo stowed in her holds had to be loaded and unloaded by using the eight cargo booms, or derricks, at the base of each mast.

Some Early Steamships

The Pyroscaphe was built in France in 1783, with a steam engine designed by James Watt. Her owner, the Marquis Claude Jouffroy d'Abbans, sailed her up the River Saone, against the current, for a quarter of an hour, but could still not find any backers.

Pyroscaphe, France, 1783

The Comet, built in Glasgow in 1812, was the first European paddle steamer to carry passengers. Her smokestack doubled as a mast, so that she could hoist a sail when the wind was favorable.

Comet, Great Britain, 1812

Robert Fulton designed and built North River of Clermont, and in 1807 sailed her up the Hudson River from New York to Albany (150 miles, or 240 km), in 32 hours. He set up the world's first successful passenger steamboat service.

North River of Clermont, USA, 1807

Sirius was the first ship to cross the Atlantic by steam power alone—but only just! In the spring of 1837 she sailed from Ireland to New York in 18½ days, but finished the voyage so short of fuel that the crew had to chop and burn the spars.

Sirius, Great Britain, 1837

Miller & Symington's
first steamboat, 1788

The Savannah, built in 1818, was the first
ship to make use of steam power on a transatlantic crossing. It took her four weeks to
sail from Savannah, in the American South,
to Liverpool, England, using steam powered
paddle wheels to supplement her sails when
necessary.

Patrick Miller and William Symington built
their first small steamboat in Scotland in
1788. Like many modern yachts, she was a
catamaran, with twin hulls. She had two
paddle wheels, sandwiched between the
hulls, one in front of the other. Fourteen
years later they built the Charlotte Dundas
for Lord Dundas of Kerse, to tow barges on
the Forth & Clyde Canal. She too, was twin-
hulled, with the boiler in one hull, the engine
in the other, and a single paddle wheel in
between.

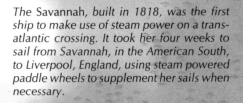

Charlotte Dundas,
Great Britain, 1802

Savannah, USA, 1818

The Far West is typical of the elegant, flat-bottomed paddle
steamers that sailed the Mississippi River at the start of this
century. They were nicknamed the river queens. Like many of
her sister ships, Far West was eventually destroyed by fire.

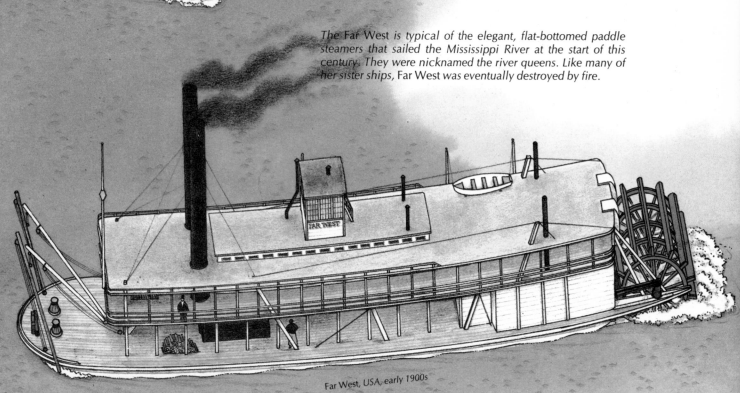

Far West, USA, early 1900s

More Powered Vessels

Cunard's transatlantic ocean liner Mauretania was nicknamed "the Grand Old Lady of the Atlantic." Between 1907 and 1934, she made over 260 double crossings of the Atlantic, and was the fastest liner of her day.

Mauretania, Great Britain, 1907

Clemens Sartori, Germany, 1955

Uri, Switzerland, 1901

Clemens Sartori, a German freighter built in 1955.

Uri, built in 1901, is typical of the passenger paddle steamers used on the Swiss Lakes.

Ferryboats carry passengers, cars and even trains over wide stretches of water. This double-ended paddle wheeler, New York, is typical of many which worked in New York harbor until recently.

New York, USA, 1892

Pusher tugboat

...and barge

BACO-LINER 1

The freighter Iberia was typical of many built at the end of the 19th century. She had two masts, so that she could use sail power to supplement her engines.

Iberia, Spain, 1881

Container ships like this one carry different cargoes in separate, sealed containers, which are much easier to load and unload. This ship can carry over 500 containers, as well as 12 barges.

Baco-Liner 1, Germany

BACO-LINER

Dredgers scoop up mud and silt, to keep navigable channels clear. This is an old bucket dredger.

Dredger, Germany, 1904

Lightships mark dangerous shoals and reefs, and act as weather stations.

Blunt's Reef, lightship, moored off Cape Mendocino, California

BLUNTS

Warships, 1765 to 1969

The USS Constitution, launched in Boston in 1797, proved to be such a fine fighting ship that she was nicknamed "Old Ironsides."

HMS Victory, launched in 1765, was Admiral Nelson's flagship at Trafalgar in 1805, when the British defeated Napoleon's navy; Nelson was wounded during the battle, and died some hours later.

HMS Victory, Great Britain, 1765

USS Constitution, USA, 1797

HMS Royal Sovereign, Great Britain, 1892

The seven warships of the Royal Sovereign class, built in the late 19th century, were the first to have steel hulls.

HMS Revenge, Great Britain, 1969

Nuclear submarines, armed with ballistic nuclear missiles, patrol the seas of the world.

The ironclad warships Monitor and Merrimack met in battle on March 9, 1862, during the American Civil War.

CSS Merrimack, renamed Virginia, USA (Confederate Navy), 1862

USS Monitor, USA (Federal Navy), 1862

The German cruiser Nürnberg, built fifty years ago, carried a seaplane which was launched by catapult.

Nürnberg, Germany, 1935

MTB, Germany, 1939–45

Motor torpedo boat from World War II, capable of speeds of 44 mph (72 kmh).

Launched a year after World War II ended, and refitted in 1960, the carrier Eagle was armed with 6 missiles, and carried 30 airplanes and 6 helicopters.

ROS

HMS Eagle, Great Britain, 1946

Sailing under Water

Submarines can sail on the surface of the water, but they can also sail beneath it, through the depths of the sea. A submarine has a double hull, with ballast tanks between the inner hull and the outer one. When she is sailing on the surface, her ballast tanks are full of air. If the vent valves are opened, air escapes, and sea water rushes in at the bottom of the tanks. The submarine gets heavier; she displaces more water, and sinks. If the vent valves are closed, and compressed air is blown into the tanks, the sea water is forced out again; the submarine is lighter, and she floats upward. Besides her ballast tanks, she has trim tanks; the amount of water in these is adjusted to keep her balanced.

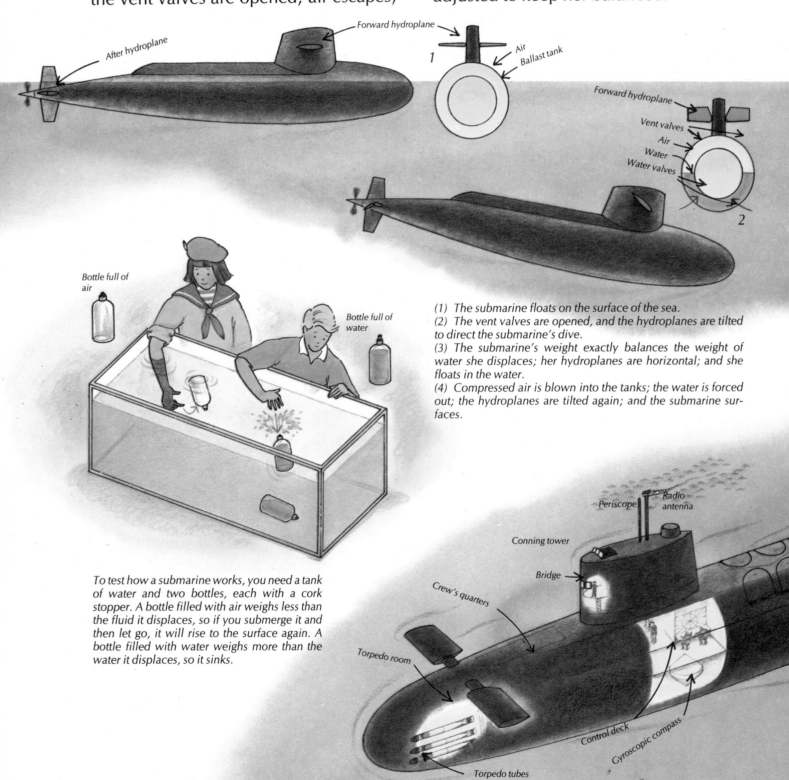

Forward hydroplane

After hydroplane

1

Air
Ballast tank

Forward hydroplane

Vent valves
Air
Water
Water valves

2

Bottle full of air

Bottle full of water

(1) The submarine floats on the surface of the sea.
(2) The vent valves are opened, and the hydroplanes are tilted to direct the submarine's dive.
(3) The submarine's weight exactly balances the weight of water she displaces; her hydroplanes are horizontal; and she floats in the water.
(4) Compressed air is blown into the tanks; the water is forced out; the hydroplanes are tilted again; and the submarine surfaces.

To test how a submarine works, you need a tank of water and two bottles, each with a cork stopper. A bottle filled with air weighs less than the fluid it displaces, so if you submerge it and then let go, it will rise to the surface again. A bottle filled with water weighs more than the water it displaces, so it sinks.

Periscope
Radio antenna

Conning tower

Bridge

Crew's quarters

Torpedo room

Control deck

Gyroscopic compass

Torpedo tubes

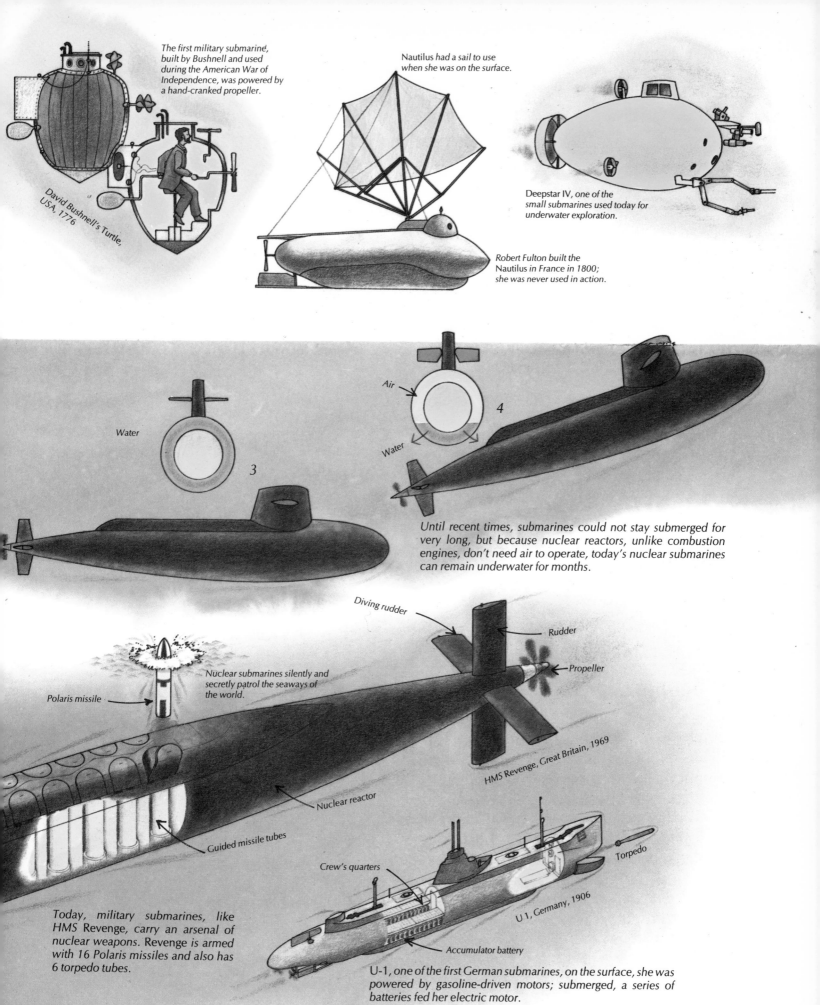

The first military submarine, built by Bushnell and used during the American War of Independence, was powered by a hand-cranked propeller.

Nautilus had a sail to use when she was on the surface.

David Bushnell's Turtle, USA, 1776

Robert Fulton built the Nautilus in France in 1800; she was never used in action.

Deepstar IV, one of the small submarines used today for underwater exploration.

Water

Air

Water

Until recent times, submarines could not stay submerged for very long, but because nuclear reactors, unlike combustion engines, don't need air to operate, today's nuclear submarines can remain underwater for months.

Diving rudder

Rudder

Propeller

Polaris missile

Nuclear submarines silently and secretly patrol the seaways of the world.

HMS Revenge, Great Britain, 1969

Nuclear reactor

Guided missile tubes

Crew's quarters

Torpedo

U 1, Germany, 1906

Accumulator battery

Today, military submarines, like HMS Revenge, carry an arsenal of nuclear weapons. Revenge is armed with 16 Polaris missiles and also has 6 torpedo tubes.

U-1, one of the first German submarines, on the surface, she was powered by gasoline-driven motors; submerged, a series of batteries fed her electric motor.

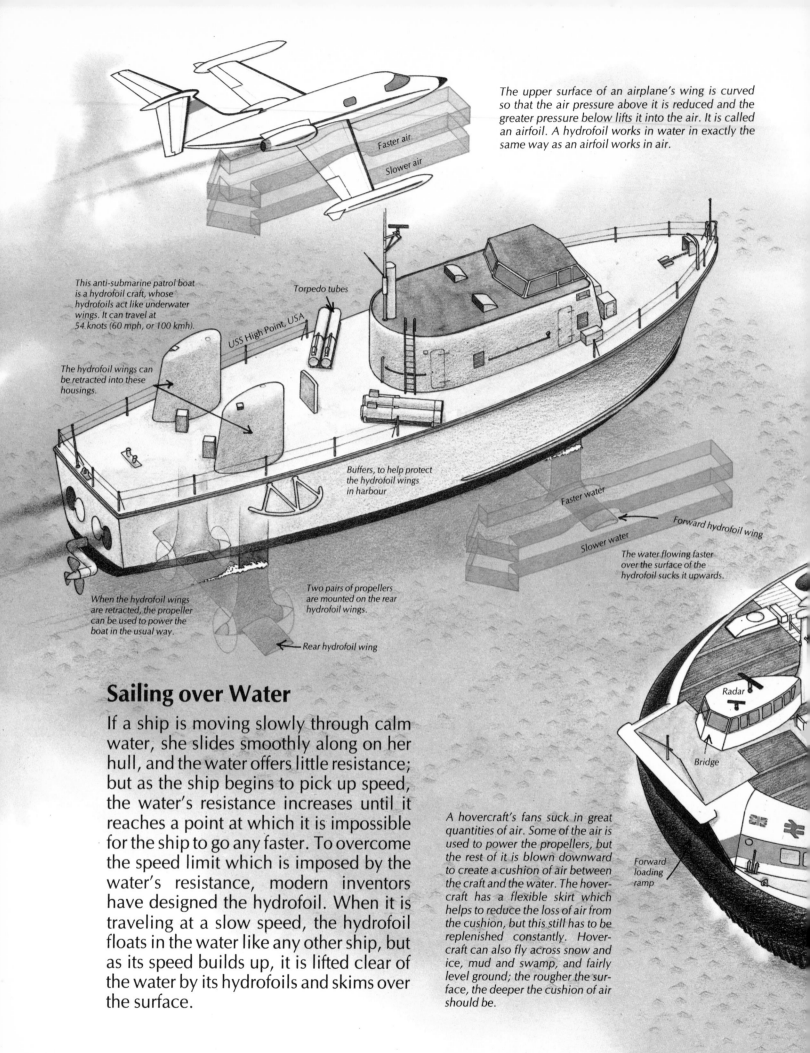

The upper surface of an airplane's wing is curved so that the air pressure above it is reduced and the greater pressure below lifts it into the air. It is called an airfoil. A hydrofoil works in water in exactly the same way as an airfoil works in air.

Faster air

Slower air

This anti-submarine patrol boat is a hydrofoil craft, whose hydrofoils act like underwater wings. It can travel at 54 knots (60 mph, or 100 kmh).

Torpedo tubes

USS High Point, USA

The hydrofoil wings can be retracted into these housings.

Buffers, to help protect the hydrofoil wings in harbour

Faster water

Forward hydrofoil wing

Slower water

The water flowing faster over the surface of the hydrofoil sucks it upwards.

When the hydrofoil wings are retracted, the propeller can be used to power the boat in the usual way.

Two pairs of propellers are mounted on the rear hydrofoil wings.

Rear hydrofoil wing

Sailing over Water

If a ship is moving slowly through calm water, she slides smoothly along on her hull, and the water offers little resistance; but as the ship begins to pick up speed, the water's resistance increases until it reaches a point at which it is impossible for the ship to go any faster. To overcome the speed limit which is imposed by the water's resistance, modern inventors have designed the hydrofoil. When it is traveling at a slow speed, the hydrofoil floats in the water like any other ship, but as its speed builds up, it is lifted clear of the water by its hydrofoils and skims over the surface.

A hovercraft's fans suck in great quantities of air. Some of the air is used to power the propellers, but the rest of it is blown downward to create a cushion of air between the craft and the water. The hover-craft has a flexible skirt which helps to reduce the loss of air from the cushion, but this still has to be replenished constantly. Hover-craft can also fly across snow and ice, mud and swamp, and fairly level ground; the rougher the sur-face, the deeper the cushion of air should be.

Radar

Bridge

Forward loading ramp

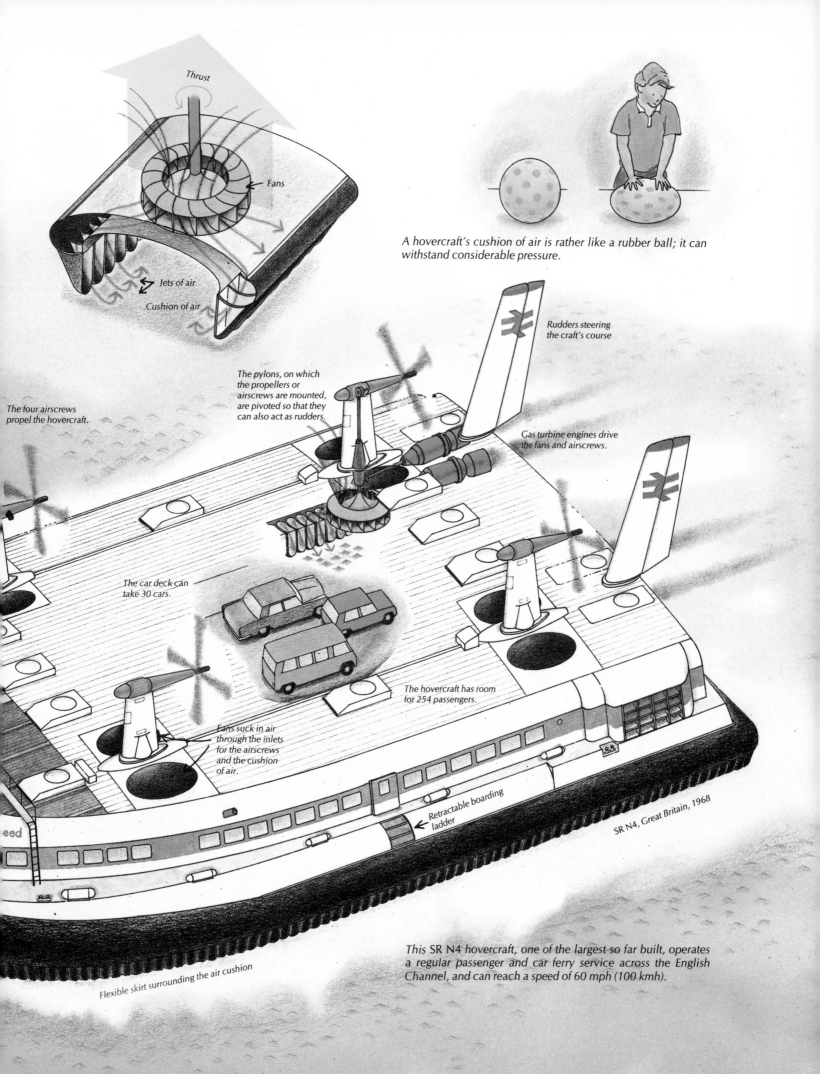

Thrust

Fans

Jets of air

Cushion of air

A hovercraft's cushion of air is rather like a rubber ball; it can withstand considerable pressure.

Rudders steering the craft's course

The pylons, on which the propellers or airscrews are mounted, are pivoted so that they can also act as rudders.

Gas turbine engines drive the fans and airscrews.

The four airscrews propel the hovercraft.

The car deck can take 30 cars.

The hovercraft has room for 254 passengers.

Fans suck in air through the inlets for the airscrews and the cushion of air.

Retractable boarding ladder

SR N4, Great Britain, 1968

Flexible skirt surrounding the air cushion

This SR N4 hovercraft, one of the largest so far built, operates a regular passenger and car ferry service across the English Channel, and can reach a speed of 60 mph (100 kmh).

Crossing Dry Land

Ships do not only sail the seas. Most of the Earth's continents are drained by great rivers flowing to the sea, and ships can often sail inland, if the river is wide and deep.

As well as the rivers, there are canals which have been dug out and filled with water to make waterways between ports and towns. Ships cannot sail uphill, so wherever rivers or canals cross land that isn't level, systems of locks have been built.

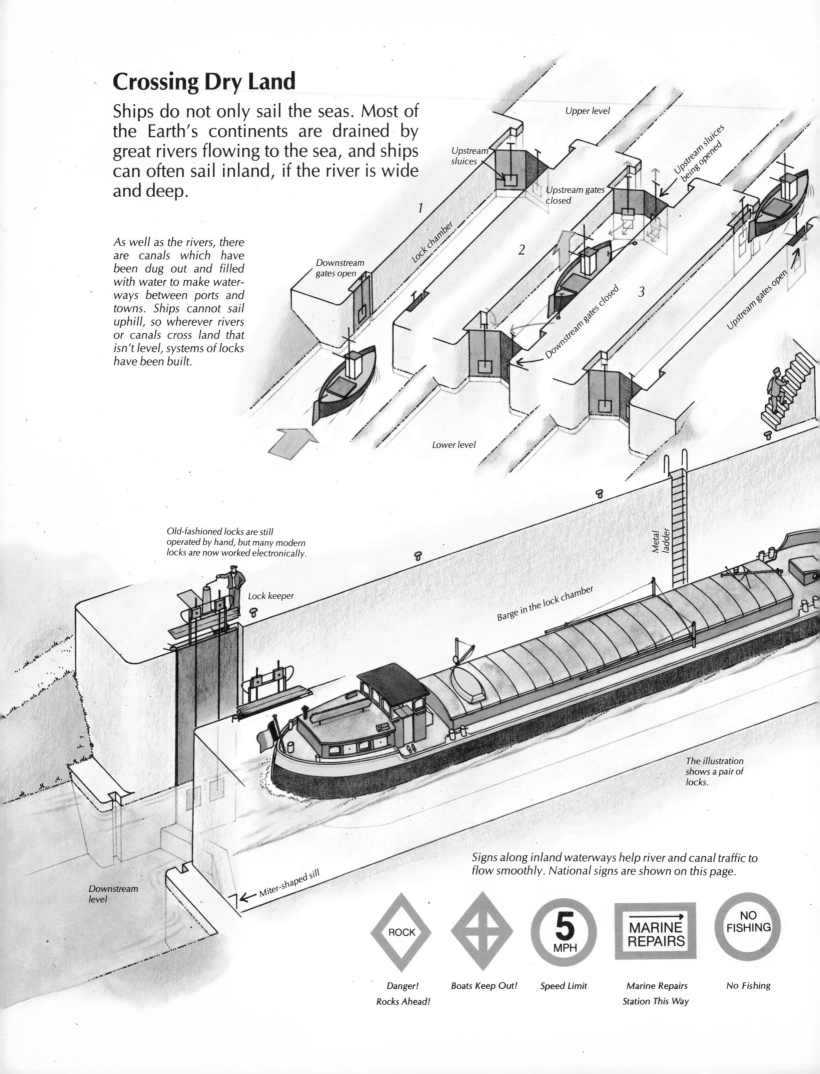

Upper level

Upstream sluices

Upstream gates closed

Upstream sluices being opened

1

Lock chamber

Downstream gates open

2

3

Downstream gates closed

Upstream gates open

Lower level

Old-fashioned locks are still operated by hand, but many modern locks are now worked electronically.

Lock keeper

Metal ladder

Barge in the lock chamber

The illustration shows a pair of locks.

Downstream level

Miter-shaped sill

Signs along inland waterways help river and canal traffic to flow smoothly. National signs are shown on this page.

ROCK

Danger!
Rocks Ahead!

Boats Keep Out!

5 MPH

Speed Limit

MARINE REPAIRS

Marine Repairs
Station This Way

NO FISHING

No Fishing

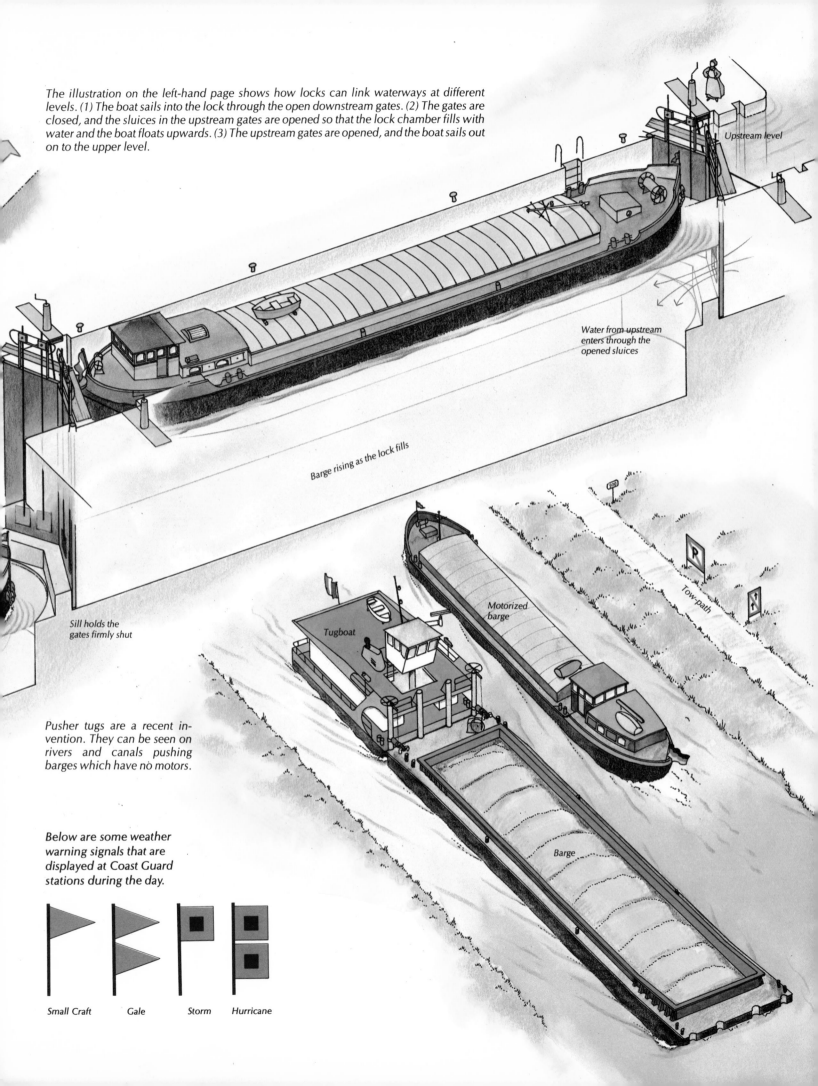

The illustration on the left-hand page shows how locks can link waterways at different levels. (1) The boat sails into the lock through the open downstream gates. (2) The gates are closed, and the sluices in the upstream gates are opened so that the lock chamber fills with water and the boat floats upwards. (3) The upstream gates are opened, and the boat sails out on to the upper level.

Upstream level

Water from upstream enters through the opened sluices

Barge rising as the lock fills

Sill holds the gates firmly shut

Pusher tugs are a recent invention. They can be seen on rivers and canals pushing barges which have no motors.

Tugboat

Motorized barge

Tow-path

Barge

Below are some weather warning signals that are displayed at Coast Guard stations during the day.

Small Craft   Gale   Storm   Hurricane

Finding the Way

When seamen first ventured into the open sea, out of sight of land, they steered by using the stars. The positions of some stars change hardly at all during the night hours, so if a sailor picked out the Pole Star and kept it at about the same point—say, just to one side of the prow—the ship would sail a straight course all night long. But this didn't work, of course, in bad weather, or by daylight, when men had to rely on the sun as it traveled across the heavens from rising to setting.

At home there are familiar landmarks to help you find your way, street signs you can read, people you can ask. But at sea there are no such aids. Whichever way you look, you can see only sky and water. Sailors find their way by using the science of navigation.

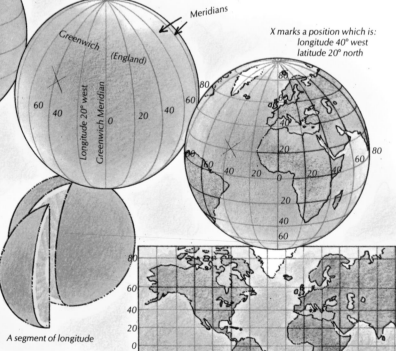

In familiar waters, not too far out, a sailor can work out his position and course if he has charts, tide-tables, a magnetic compass, a patent log (measuring the distance the ship covers), and a leadline (measuring the depth of the water). Deep sea navigation is more complicated.

X marks a position which is: longitude 40° west latitude 20° north

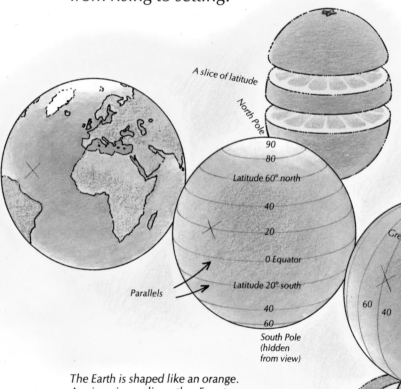

A slice of latitude

North Pole

90
80
Latitude 60° north
40
20
0 Equator
Latitude 20° south
40
60

South Pole (hidden from view)

Parallels

Greenwich (England)

Meridians

Longitude 20° west   Greenwich Meridian

60   40   0   20   40

A segment of longitude

The Earth is shaped like an orange. An imaginary line, the Equator, marks the circumference. Navigators divide the Earth into sections, using lines of latitude (parallels) which are parallel to the Equator, and lines of longitude (meridians) which run lengthways, passing through the North and South Poles. They are measured in degrees. The Equator is 0°, and so is the prime meridian which passes through Greenwich.

Meridians and parallels are shown on maps, criss crossing the world. Any point can be fixed by reference to them. Because a flat, oblong map cannot re-create the curves of the Earth's surface, the map-maker projects it. This map uses Mercator's Projection.

180 160 140 120 100 80 60 40 20 0 20 40 60 80 100 120 140 1

Because the Earth rotates once in each twenty-four hours, the time of day differs depending on where in the world you are. A navigator needs to know the difference between local time and time at Greenwich. For example, if it is seven o'clock in the morning at Greenwich, and five o'clock in the morning where you are, your longitude is 30° west. The Earth rotates once in twenty-four hours, turning through a complete circle of 360°, so in two hours it will turn 30°.

Clock

The angle of a star above the horizon varies according to the latitude of the observer.

A navigator can fix his latitude by measuring the angle at which a star is above the horizon. This measurement is usually done by using a sextant, which is a very precise instrument. A sextant, charts, mathematical tables, an almanac, a pair of compasses, a pencil and a compass are the tools of the navigator's trade.

The Earth itself is a magnet with a magnetic north pole and a magnetic south pole close to (but not at) the North and South Poles. The needle in a magnetic compass is magnetized so that it points towards magnetic north. The navigator using it must allow for the difference between true north and magnetic north. With a modern gyro-compass, this is no longer necessary.

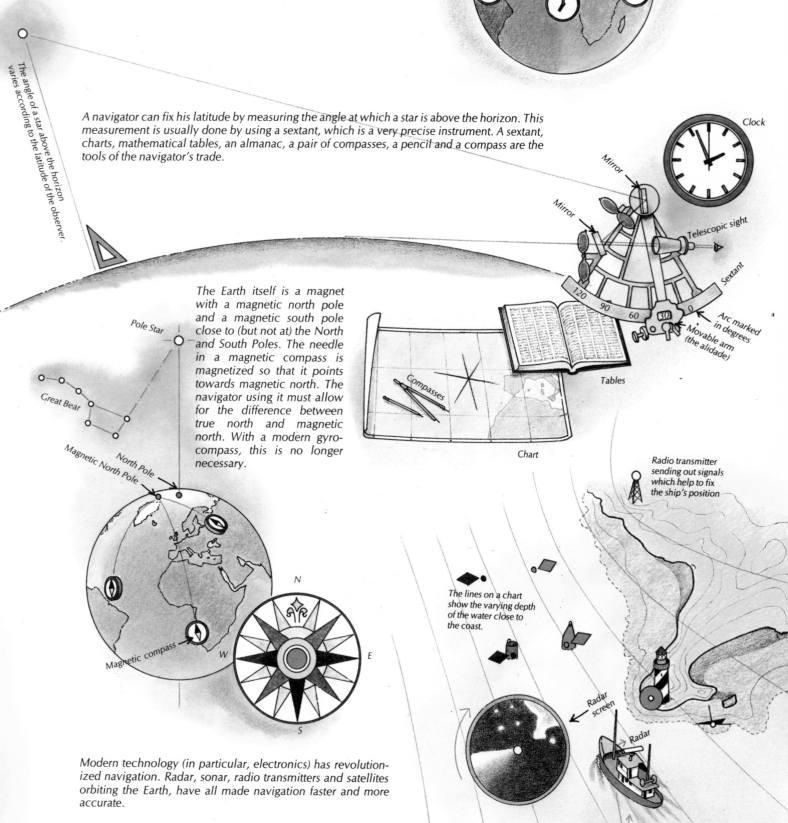

Clock

Mirror
Mirror
Telescopic sight
Sextant
120 90 60 30 0
Arc marked in degrees
Movable arm (the alidade)
Tables

Pole Star
Great Bear
Magnetic North Pole
North Pole
Compasses
Chart

Radio transmitter sending out signals which help to fix the ship's position

The lines on a chart show the varying depth of the water close to the coast.

Magnetic compass

N
W   E
S

Radar screen
Radar

Modern technology (in particular, electronics) has revolutionized navigation. Radar, sonar, radio transmitters and satellites orbiting the Earth, have all made navigation faster and more accurate.

Sonar measures the depth of water below the keel.

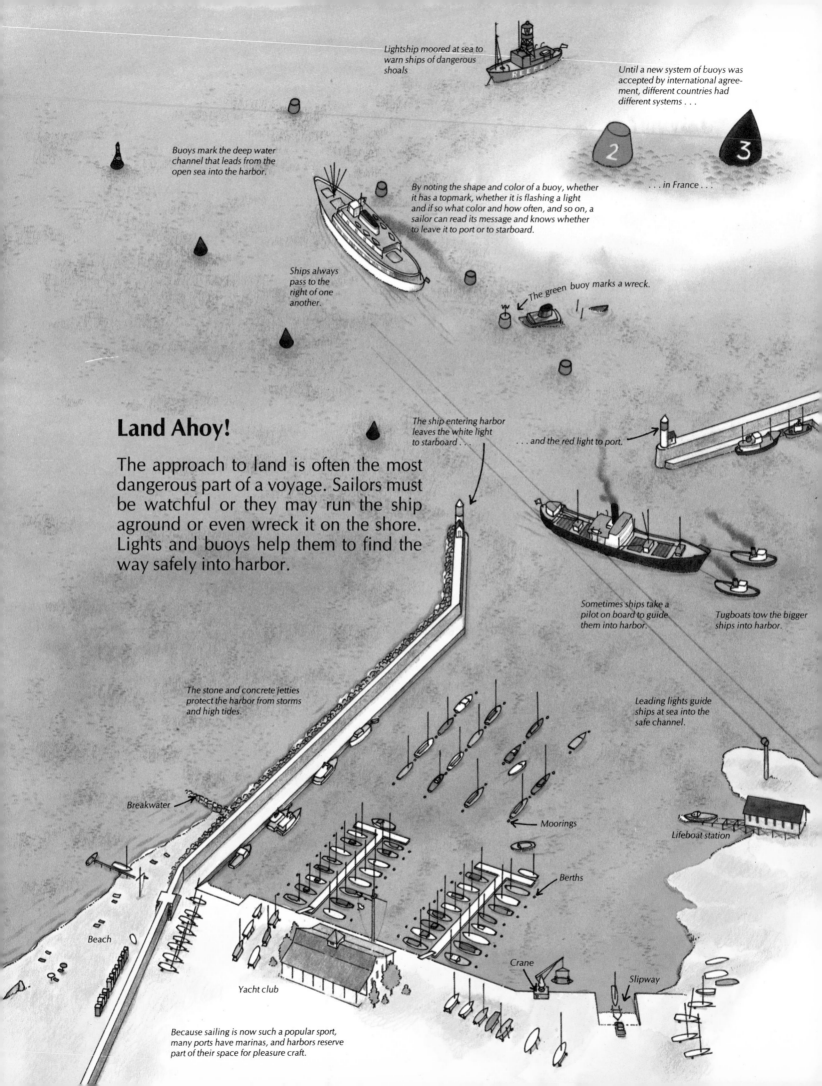

Lightship moored at sea to warn ships of dangerous shoals

Until a new system of buoys was accepted by international agreement, different countries had different systems . . .

Buoys mark the deep water channel that leads from the open sea into the harbor.

2

3

. . . in France . . .

By noting the shape and color of a buoy, whether it has a topmark, whether it is flashing a light and if so what color and how often, and so on, a sailor can read its message and knows whether to leave it to port or to starboard.

Ships always pass to the right of one another.

The green buoy marks a wreck.

Land Ahoy!

The approach to land is often the most dangerous part of a voyage. Sailors must be watchful or they may run the ship aground or even wreck it on the shore. Lights and buoys help them to find the way safely into harbor.

The ship entering harbor leaves the white light to starboard . . .

. . . and the red light to port.

Sometimes ships take a pilot on board to guide them into harbor.

Tugboats tow the bigger ships into harbor.

The stone and concrete jetties protect the harbor from storms and high tides.

Leading lights guide ships at sea into the safe channel.

Breakwater

Moorings

Lifeboat station

Berths

Beach

Crane

Slipway

Yacht club

Because sailing is now such a popular sport, many ports have marinas, and harbors reserve part of their space for pleasure craft.

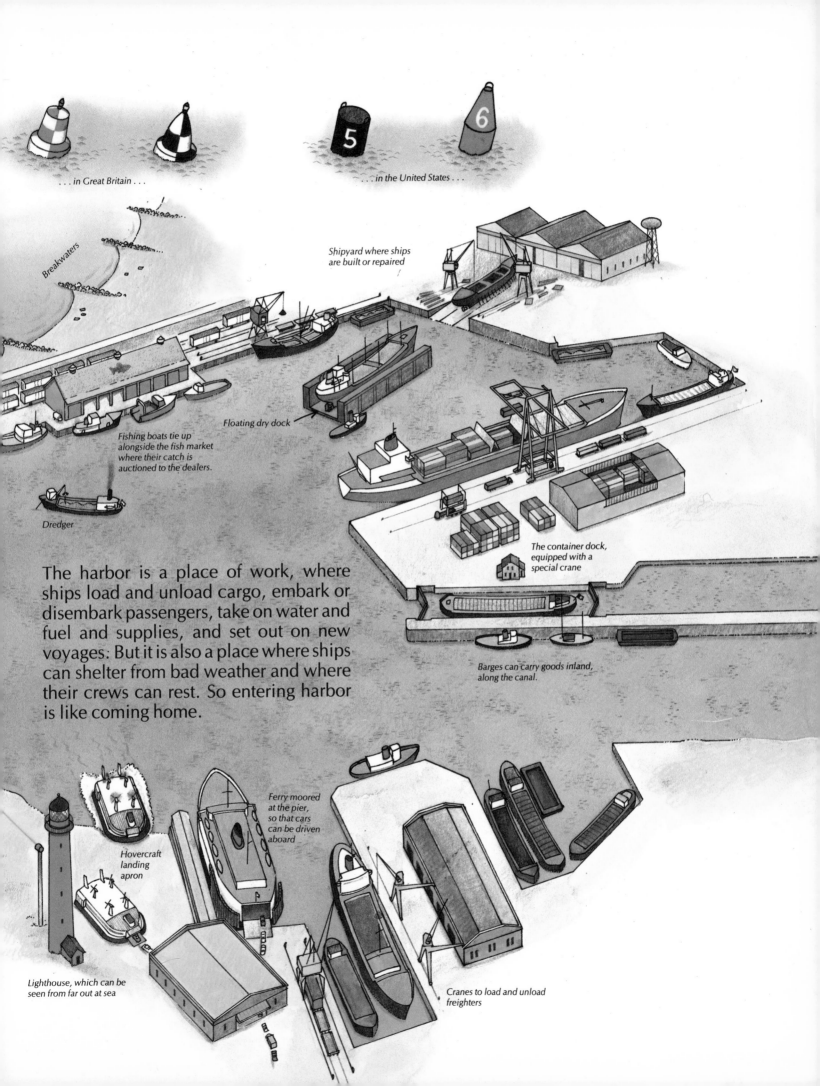

. . . in Great Britain . . .

. . . in the United States . . .

Breakwaters

Shipyard where ships are built or repaired

Floating dry dock

Fishing boats tie up alongside the fish market where their catch is auctioned to the dealers.

Dredger

The container dock, equipped with a special crane

The harbor is a place of work, where ships load and unload cargo, embark or disembark passengers, take on water and fuel and supplies, and set out on new voyages. But it is also a place where ships can shelter from bad weather and where their crews can rest. So entering harbor is like coming home.

Barges can carry goods inland, along the canal.

Ferry moored at the pier, so that cars can be driven aboard

Hovercraft landing apron

Lighthouse, which can be seen from far out at sea

Cranes to load and unload freighters